A VOICE FOR THE EVERGLADES

MARJORY STONEMAN DOUGLAS

Vicki Conrad

illustrated by **Ibon Adarne** and **Rachel Yew**

Albert Whitman & Company
Chicago, Illinois

Long ago a trickle of water
spilled from a lake
and formed a tiny stream.

This is the stream that spread far and wide,
covering nearly half of Florida.
A shallow lake that ran like a river,
so slightly,
so slowly,
no one could tell.
A river bursting with wildlife,
whispering to the world
to listen, to notice, to discover its wonders.

This is the saw grass that grows in the water.
Growing and dying,
over and over,
becoming the soil to feed the trees.

These are the trees that grow in the soil,
mangroves and cypresses,
thriving in the salty water.

This is the rainbow of birds
wading on legs like stilts,
under the shelter of the mangrove branches,
hunting for fish among the roots.

These are the Everglades.

The wildest, richest, and most diverse ecosystem in all the world—

every plant and animal needing another to survive.

The saw grass needs the water;

the birds need the fish;

the orchids need the trees;

the reptiles need the mangrove forests.

From the marshlands to the coast, it is all connected.

These are the leaders in Florida
when Miami was young—
dreaming of turning water into land,
and land into dollars.

Leaders who could not hear
the voice of the water.

These are the pumps, dams, and drains,
removing the water, creating farmland.

This is the farmland, dry and on fire,
desperate for the water it once had.

These are animals
forced to flee,
or else starve
when the water goes away.

This is an ecosystem desperate for a voice
to protect them.

This is Marjory,
a young woman
    with a sharp mind,
helping hands,
and a mighty voice.
She traveled by train from
Massachusetts to Florida,
saw the blue bays of ocean
    sparkling in the sun,
and knew she was home.

This is Marjory with Ernest,
friends paddling through saw grass,
past cypress knees
breathing for the water-soaked trees.
Friends watching whirling wheels
    of white birds dance in the Everglades.
Friends whose voices would ring out
        to protect the birds,
            the panthers,
                the trees,
                    and the saw grass.

These are friends who saw treasure, not swamp.
Who thought of the unthinkable,
Everglades National Park.

These are the Everglades—
no canyons,
mountains, or geysers.
The grandeur was in nine ecosystems.
Every animal from plankton to panther—
alligator, heron, dragonfly, turtle, manatee, dolphin, bobcat—
lived in this wild place.

This is Marjory wondering, asking,
    what are the Everglades?
This is Marjory with a huge map
    on her wall, studying their formation.
The water flowed south with ridges
    on each side. It was formed like a river—
"A river of grass," she called it.

Ernest wrote a bill,
    but worried it would fail.
Marjory wrote a poem,
    hopeful it would move Congress.

This is the battle of voices debating the national park.

"Without the Everglades, the whole nature and history of south Florida would be utterly different."

"Vile swamp! Poisonous lagoons!"

"There are no other Everglades in the world. Nothing anywhere else is like them."

"Full of filth and slimy vermin!"

"There are animals in the world that are worth protecting."

"My kids can't play in a swamp."

"The Everglades is a test. If we pass it, we might get to keep the planet."

"Huge, dismal marshes!"

"There will be no park in the world so unique, so different, so rarely beautiful."

These are the lawmakers
touring the Everglades,
seeing the water dotted with birds.
Boating through Florida Bay, Cape Sable, and Shark River,
they sailed past porpoises,
a flock of egrets and white ibis, and walls of mangroves.

The lawmakers were spellbound.
Marjory and Ernest's hopes soared.
But the bill did not pass.

This is Marjory
typing her knowledge and love
for this wild place
onto page after page.

This is her book,
The Everglades: River of Grass.

The book that turned the tide.

"*The miracle of light pours over the green and brown expanse
of saw grass and of water, shining and slowly moving,
the grass and water that is the meaning and the central fact
of the Everglades. It is a river of grass.*"

Reading her words,
people began to see...

The manatee munching seagrass,
protecting her calf from harm.

The alligator waiting by her eggs,
ready to carry her young to safety.

The red-bellied turtle,
laying eggs in the abandoned alligator nest,
dry and protected from water.

The snail kite nesting in hardwood hammocks,
hatching chicks that will grow up
to nest in their birthplace.

The only place in the world
where an alligator and a crocodile
live together.

Finally, the river was heard.

This is Everglades National Park.
The first park created to protect an ecosystem—
to preserve the plants, animals, and insects.

Yet only one-fourth of the Everglades was protected.

All the ecosystems needed one another.

Ernest kept speaking for the Everglades protection until the end of his life.

Now, Marjory was the single voice of the river.

These are the plans to build the world's largest airport, in the Everglades—
to turn trees into concrete.

This is Marjory,
eighty years old,
nearly blind.
What could she do alone?
Could her lone voice become a chorus?

These are the Friends of the Everglades,
the organization that started with Marjory
and became three thousand strong.

This is Marjory fighting to save her river of grass
from becoming miles of runways.

SAVE THE EVER-GLADES

SAVE
THE
EVER-
GLADES

*"No matter how poor my eyes are, I can still talk…
Whoever wants me to talk, I'll come over and tell them
about the necessity of preserving the Everglades."*

President Nixon listened.
Building stopped.

This is the single runway
built in the Big Cypress Forest.
A reminder of what was almost lost
and what was kept.

The New York Times

Against All Odds, the Birds Have Won

The Friends of the Everglades

arjory Stoneman Douglas
PRESIDENT

This is Marjory
educating and rallying for the Everglades,
facing boos and insults.
"Butterfly catcher! Bird-watcher!"
"Boo louder!" she answered back.

This is Marjory, ninety-nine years old,
restoring the Everglades,
chipping away the first piece of concrete
to remove a drain,
hoping the water would flow again.

This is Marjory one year later,
floating in a boat where dry land had been.

This is Marjory turning 105 years old,
winner of the Presidential Medal of Freedom.
All of Florida knew her voice.
The school children wrote her cards.
"Thank you for saving the Everglades."
"Oh, the Everglades are not saved,"
　　　Marjory responded.
She knew there was more work to be done.

These are the birds
that flocked and sang
to celebrate Marjory.

These are the Everglades,
listening for the next voice
of the river of grass.

Red-winged
blackbird

Cypresses

The Everglades Ecosystem

The Everglades ecosystem is one of the most biodiverse on Earth. There are no other water formations like it. In fact, the Everglades are made up of nine different habitats: pineland, mangrove, hardwood hammock, coastal lowland, freshwater slough, freshwater marl prairie, cypress, marine, and estuarine. Each one is home to its own variety of plants and animals.

Great blue
heron

Roseate
spoonbill

Snowy egret

Ghost
orchid

Saw grass

Loggerhead turtle

Manatee

Fauna of the Everglades

- The wading birds are an iconic symbol of Everglades National Park. There are around 400 species of birds in Florida, and at least 350 of them live in the Everglades.

- The great white egret is the largest of the wading birds. It is over 4 feet tall, with a wingspan of 50 inches.

- The wood stork is an indicator species in the Everglades: if it is present, then the Everglades are healthy.

- The roseate spoonbill is a large, bright-pink wading bird. The sides of its jaw are sensitive to touch. To hunt, the spoonbill sticks its head underwater, shakes its head, and snaps up anything it feels.

- The snail kite eats only the apple snail. If the apple snail disappears, so will the snail kite.

- The squirrel tree frog has large toe pads to help it climb trees, and it makes a sound like a squirrel.

- The brown-headed nuthatch is known for walking beak-first down a tree trunk carrying a twig, which it uses to pry up bark and find insects.

- The Florida panther is an elusive predator that inhabits the hardwood hammocks. The adults have tan coats, and the kittens have spotted coats to help them camouflage from predators. They are highly endangered.

- About 450 Atlantic bottlenose dolphins live in the Florida Bay. Dolphins can make 1,000 clicking noises per second. These sounds come from their blowholes; they do not have vocal cords.

- The West Indian manatee typically breathes once every five minutes. But they are able to stay underwater without breathing for 20 minutes. Young manatees will eat anything they see, including garbage. Mother manatees swim close to their young to keep them from eating anything harmful.

- The riverine grass shrimp is only 0.75 inches long and is transparent, or see-through. Even though it is nearly invisible, it is still an important food source for fish.

- There are 86 different species of dragonflies in Florida; they are pollinators as well as an important part of the food chain.

- The giant sphinx moth is highly camouflaged and pollinates many orchids. It has a wing span of 5–7 inches, about the size of a human hand.

- As caterpillars, zebra butterflies feed only on passionflower leaves, which have a very bitter taste. When a bird tries to eat the bitter-tasting butterfly or caterpillar, the birds spit them out immediately.

Flora of the Everglades

- Cypress trees can grow 100 feet tall and 3 feet wide. They grow and thrive in standing water. Their roots send up cone-shaped stumps next to the tree trunks. These are called "knees"—scientists think they stabilize the tree or help the tree breathe.

- Mangroves are one of the few trees able to thrive in salt water. They have huge root systems that can be seen above the water, providing shelter and habitat for wildlife.

- The royal palm tree has an entire area in the Everglades National Park named after it. Hurricanes often take off the tops of the trees, without disturbing the trunks. But the trees regrow quickly to their former height.

- Soldier wood trees are an endangered species. They grow a small fruit about the size of a peppercorn. When the fruit gets ripe, it explodes and sounds like a musket shot. That is why the tree is named soldier wood.

- A strangler fig begins as a vine growing on a tree. Soon it grows into a mass of twisted roots and engulfs the host tree; however it does not harm the tree.

- There are 47 species of orchids in the Everglades. The most famous and rare is the ghost orchid. It is hard to find, as it does not bloom often and only produces 1 or 2 blooms at a time. It is an air plant, or a plant that lives on trees.

Marjory Stoneman Douglas

Marjory Stoneman Douglas's life took many twists and turns. Throughout it all, she was passionate about helping others and making a difference.

Out of college she worked as a journalist, advocating for children in segregated Miami. Then after World War I, she volunteered with the Red Cross, delivering food and supplies to refugees in Europe.

But Marjory's heart was in Florida, and it was when she returned to Miami that she met Ernest Coe, who would become a lifelong friend. Together, Marjory and Ernest explored the Everglades on weekends. As they canoed through the saw grass, Marjory was always in awe of the flocks of white ibis and egrets that flew overhead. This land was wild and completely unknown. It deserved to be protected.

Marjory and Ernest talked about how to save the Everglades from development, and Ernest thought of the idea of a national park. With Marjory's help, he began proposing bills to Congress. Once, Marjory even wrote a poem about mangroves and gave a framed copy to every person voting on the bill. Their bills continued to fail, but Marjory and Ernest did not give up. They took lawmakers flying over the Everglades in a blimp, to show off the wonder and beauty they had experienced so many times.

However, it was Marjory's book *The Everglades: River of Grass*, which began to change the public's understanding of the Everglades. After it was published in 1947, masses of people realized the land was a treasure to protect, and Marjory took on the lead role in the fight to preserve it.

Her most passionate fight occurred in her later years, from the age of eighty to when she died at 108. She formed the Friends of the Everglades, which helped stop the construction of an international airport in the Everglades. When her eyesight failed, Marjory hired people to type and write for her so she could continue her advocacy.

In 1993 Marjory was awarded the Presidential Medal of Freedom—the highest US civilian honor—for her accomplishments. Five years later, Marjory passed away. As park rangers scattered her ashes among her beloved Everglades, a flock of red-winged blackbirds sang, and when the rangers finished, the birds fell silent.

Today her legacy lives on. The Marjory Stoneman Douglas Biscayne Nature Center is dedicated to environmental education, and an elementary school in Miami, the Florida Department of Environmental Protection, and a high school in Parkland, Florida, all proudly bear her name.

You Can Help the Everglades!

Wherever you live in the world, you can help preserve the Everglades!
Here are some things you can do:

- Join the Backyard Bird Count. The Audubon Society needs people to spend time in nature, count birds, and report what they see. Scientists use the information to study birds, and the health of the environment. www.birdcount.org/about/

- Raise money to donate to the Everglades Foundation by having a coin drive, bake sale, or another fundraising activity. The foundation is helping to fight toxic algae blooms and ensure Floridians have clean drinking water. www.evergladesfoundation.org/give-now

- Learn more about your favorite animals who live in Everglades National Park. www.nps.gov/ever/learn/nature/animals.htm

- Join the Everglades Literacy movement and help your school become a champion school. www.evergladesliteracy.org/become-a-champion-school

Selected Sources

p. 15: Davis, Jack E. *An Everglades Providence*, 21, 37, 369, 518, 604. Athens, GA: University of Georgia, 2009.

p. 15: Douglas, Marjory Stoneman, Michael Grunwald. *The Everglades: River of Grass*, 60th anniversary ed., 5. Lanham, MD: Pineapple Press, 2007.

p. 19: Douglas. *The Everglades: River of Grass*, 5.

p. 26: Douglas, Marjory Stoneman, John Rothchild. *Voice of the River*, 230. Lanham, MD: Pineapple Press, 2014.

p. 28: Walters, Tim. "'Be a nuisance where it counts.' Without Marjory Stoneman Douglas, where would Florida Everglades be?" *Florida Today*, Nov. 25, 2020.

p. 30: Lipske, Michael. "She Helped Americans Fall in Love with Florida's Everglades." *National Wildlife Federation*, April 1, 2000.

To Marjory Stoneman Douglas,
the Friends of the Everglades,
the Audubon Society,
and Everglades National Park.

Thank you for being the voice of the river.

—VC

For my friend, Elisa Fernandes-McDade

—RY

Library of Congress Cataloging-in-Publication data is on file with the publisher.
Text copyright © 2021 by Vicki Conrad
Illustrations copyright © 2021 by Albert Whitman & Company
Illustrations by Ibon Adarne and Rachel Yew
First published in the United States of America in 2021 by Albert Whitman & Company
ISBN 978-0-8075-8496-5 (hardcover)
ISBN 978-0-8075-8495-8 (ebook)
Printed in China
10 9 8 7 6 5 4 3 2 1 RRD 26 25 24 23 22 21
Design by Aphelandra
For more information about Albert Whitman & Company,
visit our website at www.albertwhitman.com.

Stitch

by

Stitch

Our thanks to Cleve Jones for his life, his work, his inspiration, and for his kind assistance with this project.

In memory of Ron—first high school friend, first friend lost to AIDS—RS

For Justin, Mac, Bobby, Jeff, and John, my dear Cleveland crew—always there for me through the years and the best company on the dance floor—JC

Magination Press is a registered trademark of the American Psychological Association. Order books at maginationpress.org, or call 1-800-374-2721.

Book design by Rachel Ross
Printed by Phoenix Color, Hagerstown, MD

Library of Congress Cataloging-in-Publication Data
Names: Sanders, Rob, 1958- author. | Christoph, Jamey, 1980- illustrator.
Title: Stitch by stitch: Cleve Jones and the AIDS memorial Quilt/by Rob Sanders; illustrated by Jamey Christoph.
Description: Washington, DC : Magination Press, [2021] | "American Psychological Association." | Summary: Determined not to let history forget those who died of AIDS, activist Cleve Jones creates a memorial quilt to commemorate the lives of those lost and bring awareness to the disease. Includes a timeline and other backmatter. Identifiers: LCCN 2020055701 (print) | LCCN 2020055702 (ebook) | ISBN 9781433837395 (hardcover) | ISBN 9781433837401 (ebook)
Subjects: LCSH: Jones, Cleve—Juvenile fiction. | CYAC: Jones, Cleve—Fiction. | NAMES Project AIDS Memorial Quilt—Fiction. | AIDS (Disease)—Fiction.
Classification: LCC PZ7.S19785 St 2021 (print) | LCC PZ7.S19785 (ebook) | DDC [E]—dc23
LC record available at https://lccn.loc.gov/2020055701
LC ebook record available at https://lccn.loc.gov/2020055702

Manufactured in the United States of America
10 9 8 7 6 5 4 3 2 1

Magination Press
Books for Kids From the
American Psychological Association

Stitch by Stitch

Cleve Jones and the AIDS Memorial Quilt

by Rob Sanders   illustrated by Jamey Christoph

Magination Press · Washington, DC · American Psychological Association

Piece by piece.
Stitch by stitch.
That's how a quilt is made.

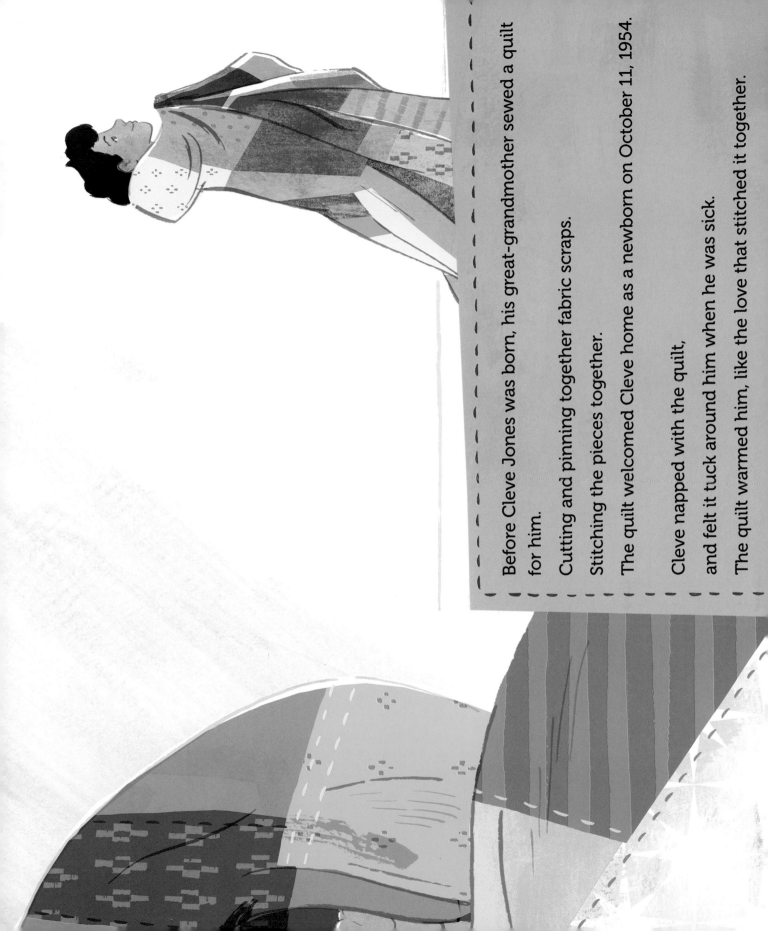

Before Cleve Jones was born, his great-grandmother sewed a quilt for him.

Cutting and pinning together fabric scraps.

Stitching the pieces together.

The quilt welcomed Cleve home as a newborn on October 11, 1954.

Cleve napped with the quilt,

and felt it tuck around him when he was sick.

The quilt warmed him, like the love that stitched it together.

As Cleve grew older, life wasn't easy for him. Even the warmth of a quilt couldn't help when he was bullied. Then things went from bad to worse.

When he was 18, Cleve told his parents he was gay.

They didn't approve.

As soon as he could, Cleve left home.

He'd heard of a place where there *might* be others like him.

A place where he *might* fit in. San Francisco, California.

One by one.
Person by person.
That's how friendships are made.

Cleve soon had
a patchwork of
friends.
They were alike
and different.

The friends were held together by a common thread.

They were people on the fringes.
On the outside.
Often without family.
Searching for acceptance.

Action by action.
Voice by voice.
That's how a movement is made.

Cleve worked for Harvey Milk.

Harvey was an openly gay politician.

A leader in San Francisco.

A mentor for Cleve.

Cleve was there when Harvey was elected to office in 1977.

Members of the LGBTQ+ community were being treated unfairly.

They weren't given the same rights as others.

Harvey, Cleve, and others in the community decided something had to be done.

Cleve went to college and started working for equal rights.

Little by little, things were changing.

Then came the day when Harvey Milk and Mayor George Moscone were assassinated.

Cleve and his friends were angry. Sad. Hurt.

Their feelings came rumbling out on the streets.

WE REMEMBER
HARVEY & GEORGE

Anger and hatred towards the community began to grow.

Progress unraveled right before their eyes.

Then things went from bad to worse.

Healthy young gay men began to be diagnosed with unusual symptoms.

Their illnesses grew worse and worse.

Most never got better.

Many died.

Pieces of the quilt of friendship were lost. Forever.

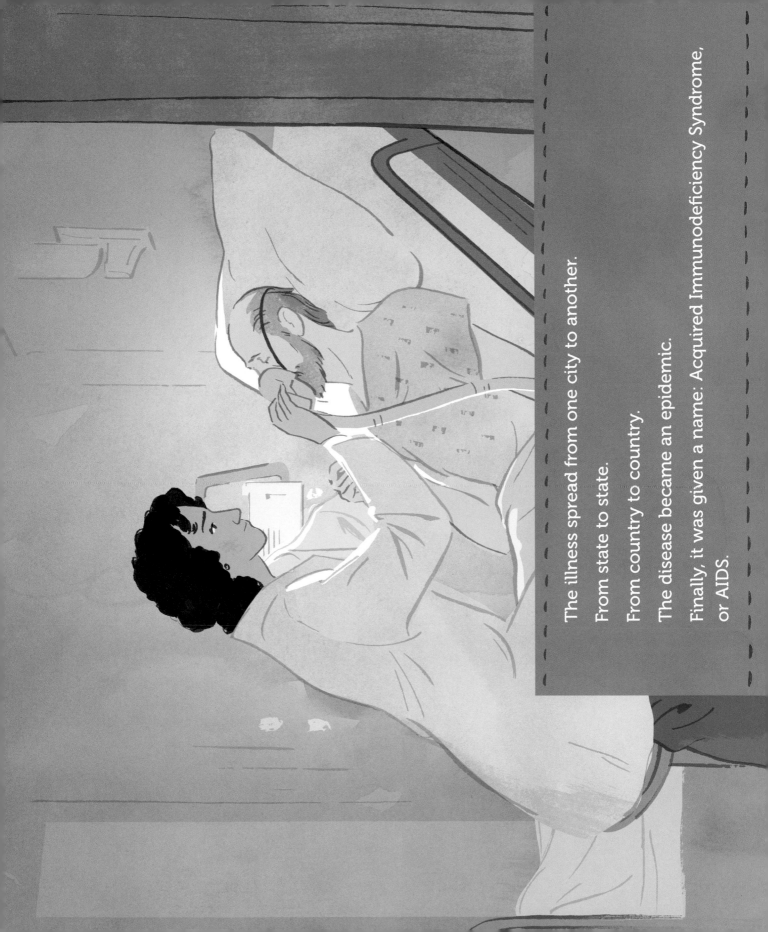

The illness spread from one city to another.

From state to state.

From country to country.

The disease became an epidemic.

Finally, it was given a name: Acquired Immunodeficiency Syndrome, or AIDS.

Most people didn't seem to care that others were dying.

Even some doctors.

Even the United States government.

Many people looked down on those with AIDS.

Some said they deserved it.

Most thought they could never get AIDS themselves.

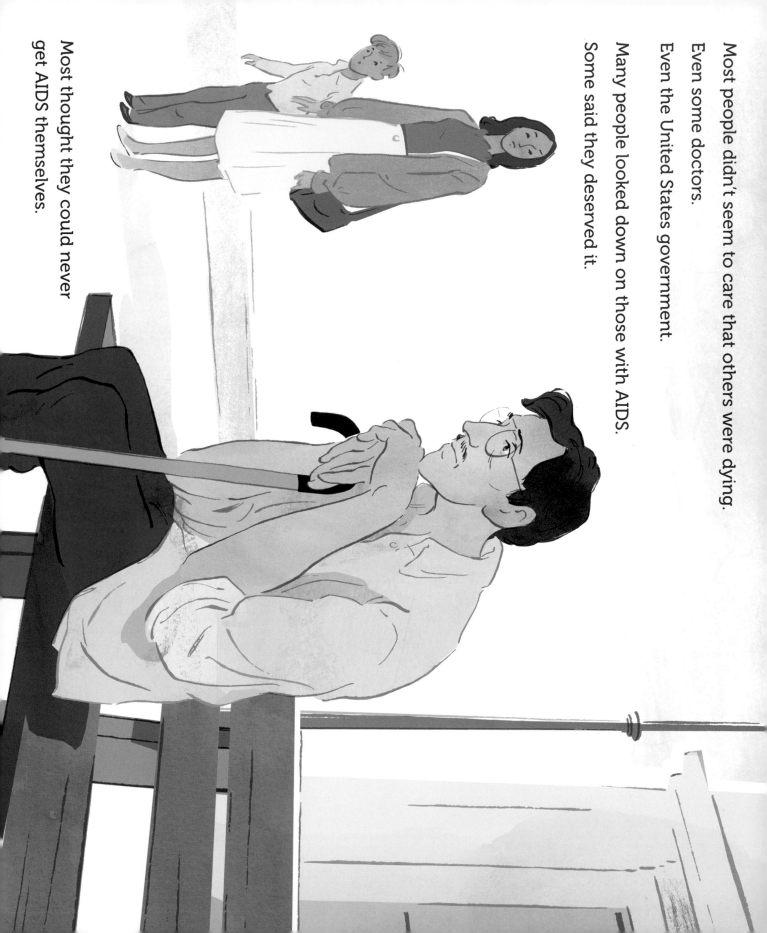

But AIDS continued to spread.

To every community.

And throughout the world.

Out of the blue.

Unexpectedly.

That's how an idea begins.

On November 27, 1985, Cleve Jones led a candlelight march to remember Harvey Milk and Mayor Moscone.

Cleve and his friend, Joseph Durant, handed out cardboard and markers.

"Write down the name of someone you know who died of AIDS," Cleve called.

Some people in the crowd wrote initials.

Some wrote only a first name.

Some wrote nothing.

Then a man took two pieces of cardboard, taped them together, and wrote his brother's full name in large letters.

Soon, others wrote the names of their friends and family members who had died because of AIDS.

One by one the names were taped to the wall of the Federal Building.

Through rain,
Cleve looked at
the names pieced
together on
the wall.

Suddenly, he had an idea.
He would create a symbol.
A memorial.
A quilt.

It took a year and a half for the idea to become a reality.

With spray paint and fabric, Cleve and Joseph created the first two Quilt panels.

Others made panels, too.

Gert McMullin volunteered to sew the panels together.

That year, during the Lesbian and Gay Pride Parade, 40 panels were displayed at City Hall in San Francisco.

News of the Quilt began to spread.

Family members and friends began to cut and pin together fabric scraps.

They stitched the pieces together, creating three-foot-by-six-foot Quilt panels.

It was a way to remember,
a way to heal,
a way to show love,
a way to do something when it seemed nothing could be done.

Slowly.

Over time.

One step at a time.

That's how change is made.

On October 11, 1987—Cleve's birthday—
squares of stitched-together panels were
unfolded and placed on the lawn of the
National Mall in Washington, DC.

The ground was quilted with names.

Each was read aloud.

The AIDS Memorial Quilt toured towns and cities.
Then things changed again.

People began to discuss AIDS.

People with AIDS began to receive help.

Money poured in for research.

Doctors began to find treatments.

The government began taking action.

Memory by memory.

Panel by panel.

That's how a memorial was made.

Today the panels on the Quilt represent 100,000 names,

100,000 individuals,

100,000 people who will be remembered forever.

Cleve called it "a monument sewn of fabric and thread."

Piece by piece.   One by one.

Action by action.   Out of the blue.

Over time.   Memory by memory.

Cleve Jones still has the quilt his great-grandmother made.

The quilt he napped with, and that tucked around him when he was sick.

It warms him to this day, like the love that stitched it together.

Cleve's first quilt inspired another—one with names.

A Quilt that remembers.

A Quilt that made a difference.

That's how a monument was sewn of fabric and thread.

Discussion Guide

When reading any book of nonfiction, questions may arise. It is also to be expected that children's questions may go deeper and deeper with each reading of a book. Create an atmosphere where children feel their questions are welcome by being honest, succinct, and by providing answers based in fact. Feel free to ask a child, "What do you think?" or "What are you feeling?" Remember, you don't have to have an answer to every question. There's nothing wrong with saying, "I don't know," or "Let me think about that." The following are some sample responses to questions that children may have after reading *Stitch by Stitch*.

Q: Is there a cure for AIDS today?

A: Since the 1980s, thanks to medical advances, medication has helped people living with HIV lead full lives. However, people who aren't treated can still die of complications caused by AIDS.

Q: How do people get HIV/AIDS?

A: HIV/AIDS is difficult to get. It is not like a cold or the flu. HIV/AIDS can be passed from person to person through unprotected sex, sharing needles, and in other ways. The most important things to know are that the transmission of HIV/AIDS can be prevented, that there are treatments if someone is diagnosed with HIV/AIDS, and that you can be friends with someone who has HIV/AIDS without worry.

Q: Was HIV/AIDS just a disease that gay men got?

A: It may have seemed that way at first, but over time doctors and scientists realized that anyone could contract the disease. Those doctors and scientists also discovered that the disease could be prevented and treated.

Q: Why didn't the government do anything about AIDS?

A: At the time, people who got HIV/AIDS were seen as people living on the fringes of society, like Cleve and his friends. Members of the LGBTQ+ community were already being discriminated against and treated unfairly. Ignoring their illness was another form of discrimination.

Q: What is discrimination and why does it happen?

A: Discrimination is the unfair treatment of people or groups of people based on who they are. People are discriminated against because of race, gender, age, sexual orientation, and other characteristics. Discrimination often is caused by fear, misunderstanding, anger, and/or hate.

Glossary

AIDS—Acquired Immunodeficiency Syndrome; a disease that attacks the immune system

assassinated—killed for political or religious reasons

epidemic—a widespread occurrence of an infectious disease

gay—used to describe a person who loves and is attracted to a person of the same gender, often used to describe men in the LGBTQ+ community

HIV—Human Immunodeficiency Virus; a virus that interferes with the body's ability to fight infections and can lead to AIDS

lesbian—a woman who loves and is attracted to other women

LGBTQ+—Lesbian, gay, bisexual, transgender, queer, or questioning. The + represents all the other identities of those in the community. When the events of this story occurred, the community was often referred to only as the gay community or the lesbian and gay community. However, those terms left out many vital members of the larger community.

on the fringes—outside of, different from, or not favored by the majority

quilt—a padded bed covering enclosed by fabric stitched in place

Cleve Jones

Cleve Jones was born on October 11, 1954 in West Lafayette, Indiana. His family moved to Scottsdale, Arizona when he was 14. After high school, Cleve attended Arizona State University. Along with his mother, Cleve was a Quaker. What he learned as a Quaker later influenced his nonviolent approach to demonstrations and civil disobedience. He came out about being gay when he turned 18. His parents did not approve. Shortly after, he moved to San Francisco, California.

Cleve quickly made friends in San Francisco and found others who were like him. He had a number of odd jobs after first moving to the city, and soon met gay-rights leader Harvey Milk. Cleve worked as a student intern in Milk's office while studying political science at San Francisco State University. Harvey and San Francisco's Mayor George Moscone were assassinated on November 27, 1978.

Cleve Jones continued his gay activism, and worked for a time in the district office of State

Assemblyman Art Agnos. In 1983, when the AIDS crisis was beginning, Cleve co-founded the San Francisco AIDS Foundation. He had the idea for what would become the NAME Project AIDS Memorial Quilt during a candlelight memorial for Harvey Milk in 1985. Cleve created the first panel for the quilt in 1987 in honor of his friend Marvin Feldman.

Cleve Jones' activism continued as he championed causes from gay rights to HIV/AIDS to marriage equality. In recent years, he has worked with UNITE HERE, a labor union of hospitality workers with a diverse membership that seeks to achieve greater equality and opportunity for its members.

Diagnosed with AIDS in the 1980s, Cleve responded well to early trials of a drug "cocktail" that fought the virus. He lives in San Francisco, California.

Meet Gert McMullin

"THE MOTHER OF THE QUILT"

When Cleve Jones called the first meeting to gather volunteers to work on the Quilt, only two people showed up. One of them was Cindi "Gert" McMullin. Initially, Gert created two Quilt panels, but she quickly became an integral part of the larger Quilt project. She was there in 1987 when the Quilt was first displayed on the National Mall in Washington, DC, she traveled to Europe for Quilt displays, and she rang Tibetan bells as the names of those memorialized on the Quilt were called—and through it all, she sewed. Gert made Quilt panels, repaired damaged ones, and sewed panels together to form the larger Quilt. Gert was given the title of Head of Quilt Production, but Cleve calls her "The Mother of the Quilt" because of the dedication and care she continues to show for it. When the headquarters for the NAMES Project AIDS Memorial Quilt was moved to Atlanta, Georgia, Gert went, too. And when the Quilt returned home to San Francisco in 2019, Gert also returned. In 2020, when another pandemic plagued the world, Gert used fabric remnants from the AIDS Memorial Quilt to make face masks. The masks were distributed in the San Francisco Bay Area. Stitch by stitch, Gert McMullin continues to make a difference.

Sources

Cleve Jones & Jeff Dawson (2000). *Stitching a Revolution: The Making of an Activist.* HarperOne.

Cleve Jones (2016). *When We Rise: My Life in the Movement.* Hachette Books.

Frontline (R), WEDU, PBS (2006, May 30). *The Age of AIDS: Interview with Cleve Jones.* http://www.pbs.org/wgbhpages/frontline/aids/interviews/jones.html

For Further Reading

Jennine Atkins (1999). *A Name on the Quilt: A Story of Remembrance.* Aladdin.

AIDS MEMORIAL QUILT TIMELINE

1985

November 27—Cleve Jones has the idea for the Quilt during a march to remember Harvey Milk and Mayor George Moscone.

1987

Cleve Jones and Joseph Durant make the first two panels of the Quilt.

June—40 panels are displayed during the Lesbian and Gay Pride Parade.

Cleve, Mike Smith, Gert McMullin, and others organize the NAMES Project Foundation.

October 11—The Quilt is displayed for the first time on the National Mall in Washington, DC. The 1,920 panels cover a space larger than the size of a football field. Half a million people visit the Quilt.

1988

Spring—The Quilt is taken on a four-month, 20-city, national tour. The Quilt triples to 6,000 panels.

October—With 8,288 panels, the Quilt is displayed on the Ellipse in front of the White House.

December 1—The first World AIDS Day is held.

1989

A second tour of North America takes the Quilt to 19 cities in the United States and Canada.

October—The Quilt is again displayed on the Ellipse in Washington, DC.

1992

Panels from every state and 28 countries are now part of the AIDS Memorial Quilt.

October—The entire Quilt is displayed in Washington, DC.

Common Threads: Stories from the Quilt is released by HBO.

1993

January—The NAMES Project marches in President Bill Clinton's inaugural parade.

1996

October—The entire AIDS Memorial Quilt is displayed for the last time in Washington, DC. The Quilt covers the National Mall. President Bill Clinton and First Lady Hillary Clinton visit the Quilt. He is the first president to do so.

2000

The NAMES Project headquarters are moved to Atlanta, Georgia.

2004

June 26—The 8,000 newest panels are displayed on The Ellipse in Washington, DC.

2019

The National AIDS Memorial becomes the permanent caretaker of the Quilt.

The Quilt returns to San Francisco, California.

Information in the section above was adapted from aidsmemorial.org/quilt-history.

LEARN MORE
To learn more about the National AIDS Memorial and the Quilt, visit aidsmemorial.org.
To experience a virtual exhibition of all 48,000 panels of the AIDS Memorial Quilt, visit aidsmemorial.org/virtual-exhibition.

THE FIRST DECADE OF AIDS IN AMERICA

1981

June—Cases of a rare lung infection and a rare, aggressive cancer are first reported in New York City and Los Angeles.

By the end of 1981, there are 337 known cases of severe immune deficiency and 130 of the cases have resulted in death.

1982

September—The CDC uses the term AIDS (Acquired Immunodeficiency Syndrome) for the first time.

December—An infant, who received blood transfusions, is diagnosed with AIDS.

A conference is held to determine guidelines for testing blood for HIV. No decision is reached.

Cases of AIDS in females are first reported.

The U.S. Congress approves funds for AIDS research and treatment.

The CDC states that HIV cannot be transferred through casual contact.

The first AIDS discrimination lawsuit is filed.

1983

1984

The cause of AIDS is discovered, and a blood test is developed to diagnose AIDS.

1985

The first commercial drug test for HIV is released.

Ryan White, an Indiana teenager with AIDS, is refused entry into school.

September 17—President Ronald Reagan mentions AIDS publicly for the first time, years after the first cases were reported.

At least one HIV case is reported in every region of the world.

Cleve Jones has the idea for a memorial quilt.

1986

The first panels of the AIDS Memorial Quilt are created.

The virus causing AIDS is officially named HIV (Human Immunodeficiency Virus).

1987

The first antiretroviral drug—AZT—is approved by the U.S. Food and Drug Administration.

The AIDS Memorial Quilt is displayed in Washington, DC for the first time.

A federal judge orders the Desoto County School Board to admit the Ray brothers—Ricky, Robert, and Randy—to school. The boys are hemophiliacs who have contracted HIV. The town is outraged, and the Rays' home is set on fire.

1988

December 1 is declared World AIDS Day.

Ryan White testifies before the President's Commission on AIDS.

The Pediatric AIDS Foundation is formed.

The first national HIV/AIDS educational program is launched.

1989

Congress creates the National Commission on AIDS.

100,000 cases of AIDS are reported in the U.S.

1990

The CDC reports the transmission of AIDS through a dental procedure.

April 8—Ryan White dies of AIDS.

Congress creates the Americans with Disabilities Act. It prohibits discrimination against people with disabilities—including HIV and AIDS.

Congress creates the Ryan White Comprehensive AIDS Resources Emergency (CARE) Act. It provides 220.5 million dollars to use for community-based care and treatment in its first year.

AZT is approved for use with pediatric AIDS.

1991

The Red Ribbon Project is launched.

By the end of the year, 160,969 cases of AIDS had been reported, resulting in 120,453 deaths.

Information in the section above was adapted from aids.gov/hiv-aids-basics/hiv-aids-101/aids-timeline and amfar.org/thirty-years-of-hiv/aids-snapshots-of-an-epidemic.

Stitch by Stitch

By Rob Sanders

Author's Note

Before this book was written, I wrote the below poem about Cleve and the AIDS Memorial Quilt. This poem is woven throughout the text of the book. Below you will find the poem in its entirety.

Piece by piece.
Stitch by stitch.
That's how a quilt is made.

One by one.
Person by person.
That's how friendships are made.

Action by action.
Voice by voice.
That's how a movement is made.

Out of the blue.
Unexpectedly.
That's how an idea begins.

Slowly.
Over time.
One step at a time.
That's how change is made.

Memory by memory.
Panel by panel.
That's how a memorial was made.

Piece by piece.
One by one.
Action by action.
Out of the blue.
Over time.
Memory by memory.